An Animal Family

DOLPHINS AND CALVES

By Mike Rodrigo-Gomez

Gareth Stevens
PUBLISHING

Please visit our website, www.garethstevens.com. For a free color catalog of all our high-quality books, call toll free 1-800-542-2595 or fax 1-877-542-2596.

Cataloging-in-Publication Data
Names: Rodrigo-Gomez, Mike.
Title: Dolphins and calves / Mike Rodrigo-Gomez.
Description: New York : Gareth Stevens Publishing, 2018. | Series: An animal family | Includes index.
Identifiers: ISBN 9781482463774 (pbk.) | ISBN 9781482463798 (library bound) | ISBN 9781482463781 (6 pack)
Subjects: LCSH: Dolphins–Juvenile literature. | Parental behavior in animals–Juvenile literature.
Classification: LCC QL737.C432 R63 2018 | DDC 599.53'4–dc23

First Edition

Published in 2018 by
Gareth Stevens Publishing
111 East 14th Street, Suite 349
New York, NY 10003

Editor: Ryan Nagelhout
Designer: Samantha DeMartin

Photo credits: Cover, p. 1 vkilikov/Shutterstock.com; p. 5 Andrea Izzotti/Shutterstock.com; pp. 7, 24 (fin) Chris Harvey/Shutterstock.com; p. 9 Willyam Bradberry/Shutterstock.com; pp. 11, 24 (pod) timsimages/Shutterstock.com; p. 13 A_Lesik/Shutterstock.com; pp. 15, 24 (calf) Wild Horizon/Universal Images Group/Getty Images; p. 17 alexytrener/Shutterstock.com; p. 19 Chase Dekker/Shutterstock.com; p. 21 marshalgonz/Shutterstock.com; p. 23 Jeff Rotman/Getty Images.

Printed in the United States of America

CPSIA compliance information: Batch #CS17GS: For further information contact Gareth Stevens, New York, New York at 1-800-542-2595.

Contents

In the Sea 4

Out of Water 8

Talk It Out 12

Playful Babies 16

Words to Know 24

Index. 24

Dolphins live in the sea.

They use fins to swim.

They love to jump.

They live in groups.
These are called pods.

They can talk
to each other!

A baby dolphin is called a calf.

They love to play.

They stay close
to the pod.

Mother dolphins take care of them.

They feed them food.

Words to Know

calf

fin

pod

Index

calf 14

dolphin 4, 14, 20

fins 6

pods 10, 18